Elfriede Möller

SHIBORI

KU-365-102

ELFRIEDE MÖLLER

SHIBORI

The art of
FABRIC TYING,
FOLDING,
PLEATING AND
DYEING

SEARCH PRESS

CONTENTS

20085477

MORAY COUNCIL
LIBRARIES &
INFORMATION SERVICES

746.66

This book is dedicated to
my daughter Anja
~

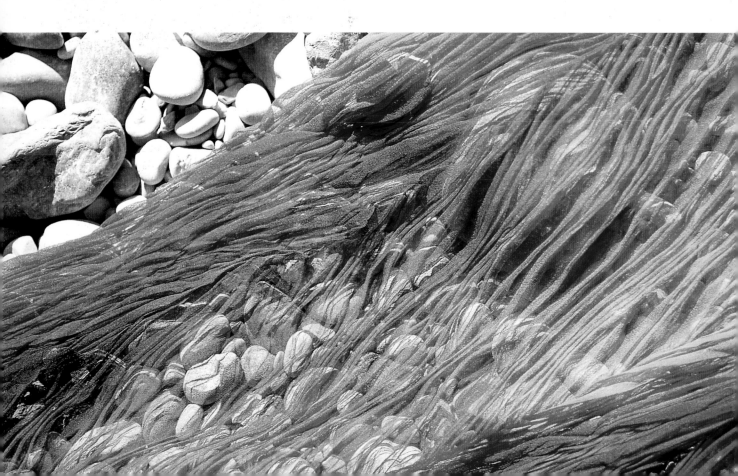

FOREWORD

I have worked with textiles for some twenty years and my enthusiasm is constantly rekindled by the wide range of possibilities that they offer the artist. Textile artists, especially silk painters, often work with techniques which produce clear lines. I, however, have broken away from these rigid forms. I am constantly looking for new methods of working and I try to keep my eyes open to the many stimuli offered by the world around us — I then integrate as much as possible into my own work.

In the past, it has often been new fabrics which have challenged me to invent innovative techniques or to enrich established methods with fresh ideas. When I discovered the centuries-old craft of shibori, I soon realised it provided an ideal method for manipulating and altering fabrics. It is a wonderful technique, which allows chance to intervene again and again, yet at the same time, decisions can be taken during the process which help determine the outcome.

I had my first encounter with shibori in Julie's Gallery, the textile gallery in New York. I gazed in fascination and admiration at the finely patterned fabrics, scarves, drapes and clothes. I immediately purchased a book about shibori and enroled on a workshop with Carter Smith, a shibori expert from Boston. There was now no

stopping me. What followed was a period of experimentation, until I finally achieved the effects I was looking for.

This book is an attempt to adapt traditional shibori techniques, combine them with more contemporary methods, and then apply them to modern fabrics — in other words, the principles of silk painting are combined with elements of shibori. Mixing these techniques opens up an exciting world full of fabulous colour, pattern and texture.

I try to pass my enthusiasm on to students who attend my courses and I share their joy when they excitedly, and with some amazement, unfold their work. I hope that this book will allow you to experience a similar fascination and delight. So, prepare to be surprised as you dip into the world of shibori, and the magic of transformation . . .

Elfriede Möller

5

WHAT IS SHIBORI?

Shibori is a form of tie-dyeing which originates in Japan. Unlike fabric painting and fabric printing, areas of the fabric are folded, wrapped, twisted or pleated in special ways and then secured with string. The fabric is then dyed. When untied or unwound, unique patterns emerge.

Shibori, and similar dyeing processes, are used not only in Japan, but also in China, India, Indonesia, Africa and Latin America. Shibori is also related to the tradition of indigo dyeing which is known in Europe and widespread in Sweden, Denmark, Hungary and Slovakia.

It is suspected that shibori culture originated in China. Archeological excavations have revealed frescoes on which shibori fabrics can be identified. In present day China, however, there are only a few regions in which shibori is known to be practised.

Japan, on the other hand, has a living tradition. The oldest finds there go back to the seventh and eighth centuries AD. It was in the sixteenth and eighteenth centuries that shibori techniques were refined — the result was a greater virtuosity and precision in the craft. Traditional methods were improved upon, superseded by new ones and craftsmanship matured to its highest level of perfection. New terms subsequently appeared for the various versions of shibori.

The shibori tradition originates from oriental culture.

In Japan, shibori was, and still is, well known and popular. The production and decoration of fabrics is closely bound up with Japanese culture. This may explain the durability of these processes, which, despite industrialisation, are still used in many commercial enterprises up to the present day. Since the end of the seventies, shibori has been taught once again in Art Colleges in Japan, so as not to allow these old traditions to fall into oblivion.

MATERIALS

Fabrics

I have used the following fabrics for the designs featured in this book. All these fabrics are obtainable by the length, cut from a roll, from fabric or silk-painting shops. You can also use ready-made items (i.e. cut out and hemmed), such as scarves.

Silk chiffon A transparent, delicate fabric with a plain weave.

Satin crêpe This fabric has a light, soft, satin weave. It has a very smooth, shiny rightside and a rough, matt underside.

Silk crêpe de chine This high quality, grainy fabric has a matt lustre and a plain weave. It is crease-resistant.

Silk crêpe georgette A semi-transparent, slightly textured fabric which has a plain weave. It is similar to chiffon but heavier and much more hard-wearing.

Silk pongé This is a smooth, light fabric which has a plain weave. It comes in a variety of weights. I use a No. 05 or 06.

Velvet A mixed fabric with a pile rightside and a smooth underside. It is available in black and white. The crêpe rightside consists of viscose, the smooth underside of silk.

Velvet devoré This fabric has a pattern which is burnt into it with an acid during a special process.

Wool (wool muslin) A lightly woven fabric with a plain weave.

Silk painting dyes

There are many different types of silk paints and dyes. The paints are fixed by ironing, the dyes by steaming. Only steam-fix dyes should be used for the techniques in this book. These dyes can normally be mixed with one another to obtain other colours. The three primary colours are red, yellow and blue; all other shades can be mixed from these. The colours of dyes are usually highly concentrated, and can be diluted with water to produce pastel shades.

I have had very good results with both traditional acid and reactive dyes.

Acid dyes are acidic and mineral compound dyes. The colours produced are brilliant and vibrant and, when fixed, they are light-fast and wash-fast. An acid, such as vinegar, is used to aid and speed up dye-fixing.

Reactive dyes are synthetic and combine chemically with the fibres in the fabric. The colours are light- and wash-fast and durable. These dyes require an alkaline for fixing, such as bicarbonate of soda – this can normally be purchased with the dyes.

Some ready-mixed, liquid steam-fix dyes do not need any additional additives to aid fixing. Check the manufacturer's instructions before you begin.

For some effects, I also use non-reducible (non-dischargeable) dyes. These colours are mixed with discharge paste (see page 11).

Fixing the dyes

Fixing involves combining the dyes with the fabric to make the fabric colour-fast, wash-fast and light-fast. The task of fixing will recur frequently in this book, and is achieved either by steaming or by boiling the fabric.

The conventional steam-fixing method involves laying the fabric between two layers of protective paper (e.g. newspaper). This is then carefully wrapped up and placed in a steamer for three to four hours. Specialist shops often offer a fixing service — ask when you buy your dyes or fabric.

Silk painters will be used to fixing the painted silk once it is thoroughly dry. With the techniques shown in this book, however, steam-fixing is worked as soon as the dyes have been applied, while they are still damp.

Interim steam-fixing is a method of fixing the dye before it is boiled in a second colour — boiling would otherwise disperse the first dye colour and the pattern would be lost. This interim fixing takes only about fifteen to twenty minutes, but, even so, it is very effective — if you wash the fabric immediately afterward, you will find that virtually none of the dye runs.

With some shibori techniques, the silk or wool is boiled in a diluted dye to fix it. This process does not affect the silk, since the silk cocoon has already been boiled to kill off the caterpillar.

Nor does boiling affect wool, since wool only becomes matted if a detergent is added to the hot water, and the fabric is rubbed. In this instance the wool is simply boiled in dye and water.

After fixing, you can wash the fabric by hand as usual, then wrap it in a towel and gently squeeze out excess water. When almost dry, you can iron it. Remember, however, that you should not iron velvet.

Dyeing

There are two ways to dye fabric — either boil it in a diluted dye solution, or paint it directly on. The boiling method, also serves to fix the dyes.

METHOD 1

The amount of dye needed will depend on the shade required, but it will generally be 50–80ml of dye per litre of water (1–1½fl.oz per pint). Fill the bottom of a saucepan with water, to a level of about 10cm (4in). Bring the diluted dye to the boil, then immerse the fabric in this dye bath — you can hold it down with a wooden spoon. Boil for approximately fifteen minutes, turning the fabric frequently. Rinse in clear water, then squeeze out excess moisture with a towel.

METHOD 2

Dampen the fabric with water then stretch it on a silk-painting frame. Paint as required, then allow to dry.

Discharging

As an addition to traditional shibori, I use the discharging technique. Discharging removes or 'bleaches out' colour to leave a white pattern. It can be applied to black fabric or fabric that you have already dyed or painted. After fixing, the discharged fabric can be washed by hand without any problem. There are two distinct methods of discharging. If using method 1, remember that the dye must be fixed before you start, otherwise all the colour will wash out when the silk is rinsed after discharging. For method 2, you can mix a non-reducible dye with the discharge paste — in this way, the old colour is bleached out and a new colour is applied in its place.

Warning Always work in a well ventilated area and use rubber gloves for this technique.

METHOD 1

1. Add 1 teaspoon of discharging salt to 500ml (1 pint) of water. Heat up the mixture in a shallow dish.

2. Take the piece of fabric to be discharged (here a scarf wrapped up ready for twisting) and lay it in the bowl and turn over once. Remove once the colour has lifted to the shade you require. Rinse thoroughly.

METHOD 2

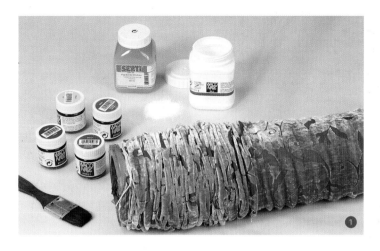

The scarf used in this demonstration is velvet which has been dyed turquoise using the boiling method. The scarf was then tacked together lengthwise and pushed on to a tube (see pages 22–23) ready for discharging. The finished scarf is pictured on page 30.

1. For this demonstration you need discharging salt, a normal commercial thickener and non-reducible dyes. Note: You do not have to add non-reducible dyes for the discharging technique. If you leave them out, the effect will be white.

2. Mix 250ml (½ pint) of thickener with 45gm (1½oz) of discharging salt. Tint the paste with non-reducible dyes, using one part paste to one part colour.

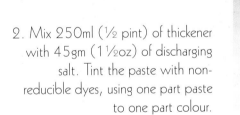

3. Apply the paste to the dry fabric using a paintbrush. Allow the fabric to dry after discharging then steam-fix. Note that it is only through the fixing process that the non-reducible dye colours become really bright.

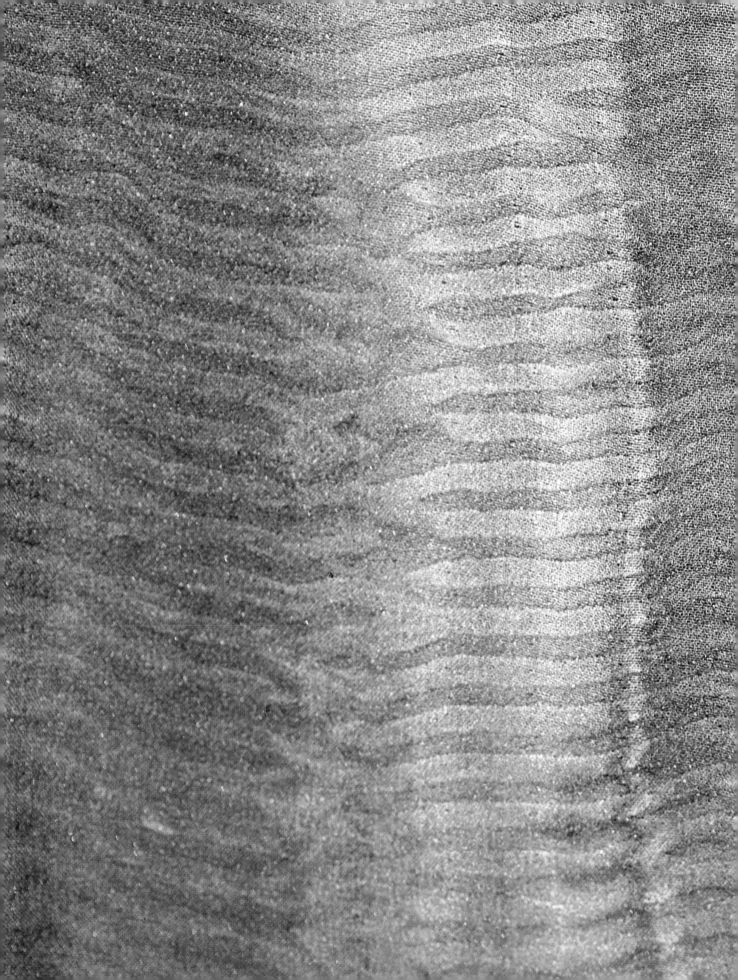

Other materials

For some techniques you will need the following additional materials:

- Cotton string and scissors
- Pipettes or pipette flasks
- Tubes (for the Arashi technique)
  a. Tube, approximately 115cm (45in) in circumference (e.g. a large plant pot)
  b. Tube, approximately 38cm (15in) in circumference (e.g. a PVC roll, plastic piping or a large bottle)
  c. Wooden dowel, about 20–25cm (8–10in) long, and 2.5–3.5cm (1–1½in) in diameter (this is also used for the Pleating technique)
- Needles and tacking thread
- Hotplate
- Steam iron
- Saucepan, about 25–30cm (10–12in) high, and 25cm (10in) diameter, with a steaming basket fitted inside
- Aluminium foil
- Plastic or metal grid (available from art and craft shops) or cake cooling rack
- Small wooden boards and clamps (for the Itajime technique)
- Rubber gloves
- Autofade marker (for the Meander technique)
- Plastic bowl or bucket (for collecting dye)
- Various sturdy paintbrushes
- Smocking pleater (for the Pleating technique)

ARASHI

All shibori techniques which are carried out on a tube or length of wood are called Arashi. A Japanese man by the name of Kanezo developed this technique at the beginning of the nineteenth century. Arashi means 'storm' and the term was first coined because it was thought that the patterns which resulted from the technique looked like rain lashed by the wind. The results surpassed all other shibori techniques, and Arashi soon became widely known.

I use three different sizes of tube for Arashi — small, medium and large. For the small tube I use a wooden dowel; for the medium tube I use a cardboard tube, around which I wrap waterproof heavy-duty adhesive tape; and for the large tube I often use a big plant pot. You could also use a PVC roll, plastic piping or even a large bottle. Have a look in your cupboards at home, or rummage around at a builders yard for something suitable. It does not matter what you use. With the exception of the wooden dowel used in the Twisting technique, the important thing is that the circumference of the tube and the width of the fabric are the same.

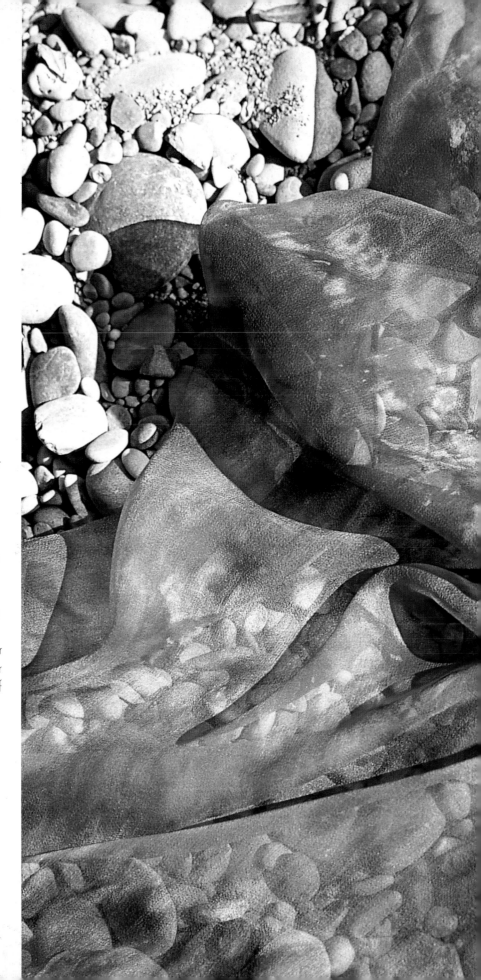

Twisting

The verb 'to twist' implies turning, wrapping or winding, but it also describes, in general terms, the flexibility of fabric. The Japanese fashion designer, Issey Miyake, called his 1992 collection 'Twist fashion'; he too, incidentally, designs from the creative realm of shibori art. The concept of 'twisting' originates from Carter Smith, a shibori expert from Boston, and it describes a special form of Arashi, in which the fabric is wrapped around a wooden dowel rather than stretched over a tube. The dowel should be about 25cm (10in) in length, with a diameter of 2.5–3.5cm (1–1½in). Here, I have used a woollen scarf, 45cm (18in) wide and 200cm (80in) long, but you could use other fabrics — silk georgette works particularly well with this technique. I have used acid dyes for the demonstration, which is why vinegar is used (see page 8).

METHOD

1. Immerse your length of fabric in water. Wring it out well and then, with the help of another person at the other end, carefully fold it lengthwise. Without either of you letting go, pull the fabric taut and then twist it to form a sturdy cord. (Note: If you use silk, you do not have to wet the fabric to begin with.)

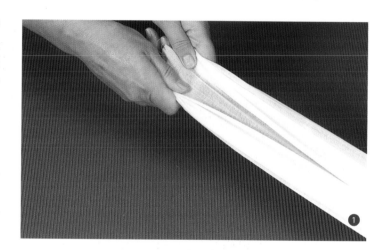

2–3. Wrap the cord around a wooden dowel and fasten it at both ends with cotton string.

16

4. Use a pipette to apply acid dyes along the length of the dowel. You could also apply the dyes around it, depending on the effect you require.

5. Place a steaming basket at the bottom of an ordinary cooking pot. Mix up a 50:50 solution of water and vinegar. Hold the dyed roll over the pot and apply this dilution with a pipette flask.

6. The fabric is now ready for the interim fixing. Add about 2.5cm (1in) of water to the bottom of the cooking pot then place on a hotplate. Lay the dyed roll in the steaming basket, cover the pot with aluminium foil and steam the fabric for twenty minutes. Now rinse the roll in water, squeeze with a towel to dry it off and finally, uncoil the fabric.

Tip With wool, I then fix according to the conventional steam-fixing method.

VARIATION

You can follow the six steps shown here but, before uncoiling the fabric, boil for eight minutes in a black dye bath — use 80ml of dye per litre of water (1½fl.oz per pint). The black-dyed fabric can then be partly discharged following method 2 on page 10. Finally, rinse thoroughly, towel dry and remove the fabric from the roll.

Woollen scarf
45 x 200cm (18 x 80in)

This impressive scarf was made by following steps 1–6 on pages 16–17.
It was coloured using acid dyes and then steam-fixed.

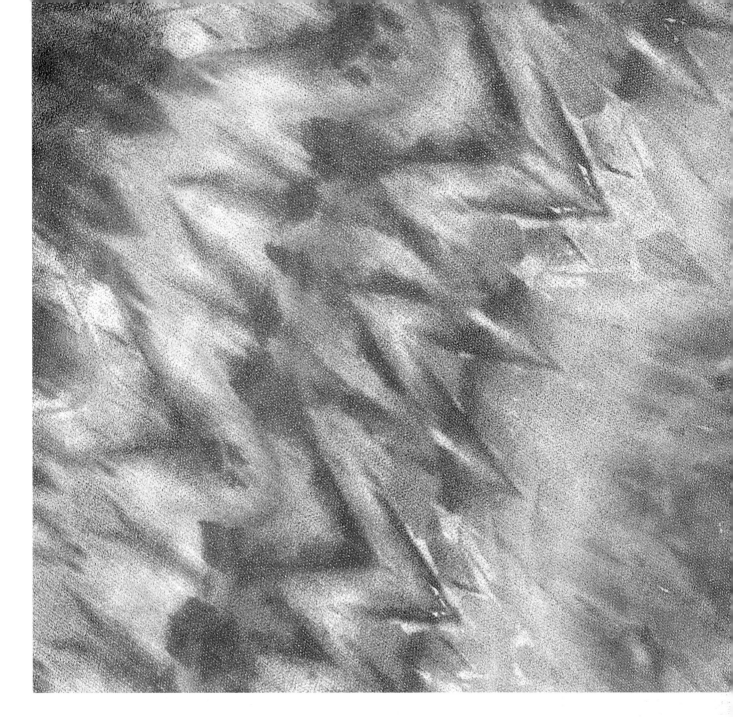

Chiffon scarf (see also illustration on pages 14–15)
115 x 200cm (45 x 80in)

This scarf was coloured using the same technique as the woollen scarf shown opposite.
This time, I used reactive dyes.

Velvet devoré scarf
180 x 90cm (72 x 36in)

In this example, I boiled the velvet scarf for twenty minutes in a
caramel-coloured dye bath. The lining is made from chiffon, and was
dyed with acid dyes, following steps 1–6 on pages 16–17.

Georgette scarf
250 x 55cm (100 x 22in)

I used acid dyes to colour this delicate scarf. After following steps 1–6 on pages 16–17, the fabric
was boiled in a black dye bath (see Variation) and then discharged using method 1 (see page 10).

Arashi on velvet

Many of my ideas and methods are often formed as a result of experimenting. It is amazing how many different variations of Arashi are possible, particularly by combining the technique with new fabrics, dyes and other processes, such as discharging. I am particularly keen on working with velvet and velvet devoré, and the Arashi technique that I have adapted here, works brilliantly with both. The beautiful dark transverse stripes appear on the velvet during the drying process. For this demonstration I have used a velvet scarf, 38 x 180cm (15 x 72in).

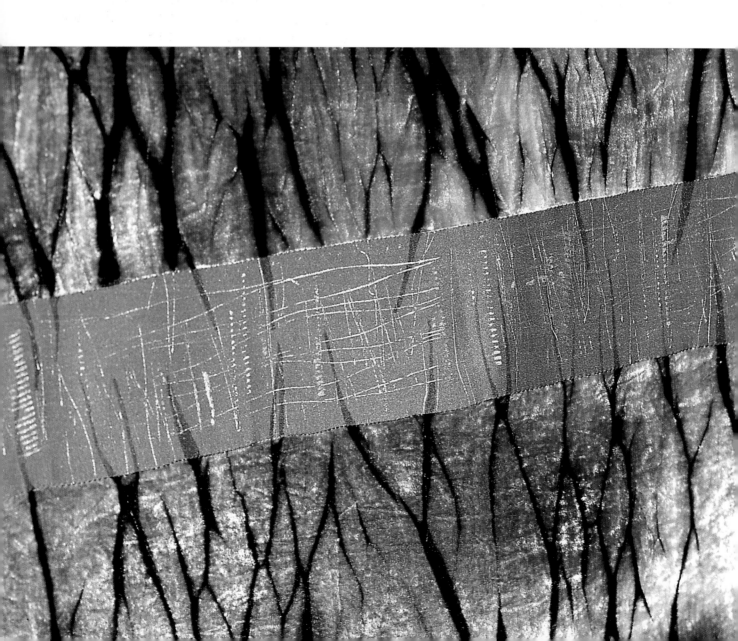

METHOD

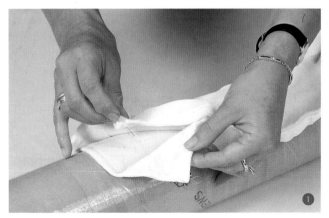

1. Tack the long edges of a velvet scarf together using large stitches.

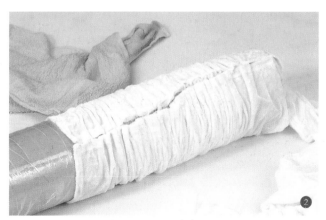

2. Immerse the scarf in water and then wring it out. Remove excess moisture with a towel. Push the damp scarf on to a 38cm (15in) circumference tube.

3. When the entire scarf is over the tube, secure one end of it to the roll with string. Now firmly push the other end up towards it, to form tiny pleats. Fasten the free end of the scarf to the tube with string then apply the desired colours with a firm paintbrush. Try to ensure that the gaps between the pleats are painted as well. It is a good idea to wear rubber gloves when doing this — then you can push the velvet apart as you work, to check that the dye has reached all areas.

4. (Not illustrated) After applying the dye, lightly dry the velvet with a hairdryer or a blower heater, then leave to dry thoroughly. Remove the velvet from the tube, then steam-fix for about four hours. Wash the scarf by hand, wring it out in a towel and leave to dry flat. Do not iron.

VARIATION

If you want to give the velvet a more pronounced, bark-like appearance, dye the fabric as described here, but then wrap the velvet in protective paper and leave it on the tube while steam-fixing for four hours. Do not remove the scarf from the tube until it has cooled right down. Do not wash.

23

Double-sided velvet scarf
180 x 38cm (72 x 15in)

This scarf was dyed following steps 1–4 on page 23. The fabulous texture was created as a result of leaving the velvet on the tube while it was steam-fixed (see Variation).

Velvet and satin crêpe travelling rug (see also detail on page 22)
200 x 140cm (80 x 55in)

This spectacular rug was coloured using acid dyes. Three strips of velvet were dyed
separately (see page 23, steps 1–4). The underside of the rug was cut out of quilted silk,
placed on a frame, painted plain green and then steam-fixed. Satin crêpe was used for the
edging and median strips, and this was dyed in the same way as the quilted silk. Once
sewn together, the green median strips were painted with gold and bronze outliner.

Velvet drape

115cm (45in) square

Subtle shades of blue, green and purple acid dyes were used to colour this fabulous drape. The velvet was sewn along the selvedges, then it was dampened and pushed over a thick tube, 115cm (45in) in circumference. It was dyed (see page 23, steps 1–4), steam-fixed and then washed. The same velvet was sewn up again, but this time along the raw edges. It was dyed as before, to produce an unusual criss-cross pattern.

Velvet devoré scarf
180 x 38cm (72 x 15in)

This double length of velvet was twisted on the tube towards the right and only then was the fabric pushed together to form tiny pleats. It was coloured using acid dyes, following steps 1–4 on page 23. The scarf was then twisted to the left and dyed as before – this produced the diagonal criss-cross pattern. The scarf was lined with chiffon, coloured with the same dyes as above, but this time using the Twisting technique shown on pages 16–17.

Velvet devoré scarf
180 x 38cm (72 x 15in)

This rainbow-coloured and richly-textured scarf was dyed using acid dyes, following steps 1–4 on page 23. The chiffon lining was coloured using the same dyes but with the Twisting technique shown on pages (see page 16–17).

Velvet devoré scarf
180 x 38cm (72 x 15in)

This scarf was placed in a turquoise dye bath and boiled for fifteen minutes. Once dry, it was sewn along the long edges and pushed on to the tube. It was then discharged using method 2 and non-reducible dyes (see pages 10–11).

Velvet scarf
180 x 38cm (72 x 15in)

This eye-catching scarf was painted on a frame using three vibrantly-coloured acid dyes (see page 10). When dry, it was sewn along the long edges and pushed on to the tube. It was discharged following the same method as the scarf above. Finally, the scarf was lined with blue silk chiffon.

Fringed velvet scarf
180 x 38cm (72 x 15in)

A fringe can transform a scarf and add the finishing touch. Here, a plain, unfringed velvet scarf was painted on a frame using four colours of acid dye (see page 10). Once dry, the scarf was sewn up along the long edges and pushed on to the tube. It was discharged using the same method as both the scarves opposite. A satin fringed scarf was dyed using acid dyes and the Twisting technique (see pages 16–17). It was then sewn on to the reverse side of the velvet scarf to provide both the fringe and the lining.

Black velvet drape
115cm (45in) square

A black velvet square was sewn along the selvedges and then pushed on to a thick tube,
(circumference 115cm (45in). It was discharged using method 2 and a combination of
no dye (to obtain a clear, colourless effect), and green dye (see page 11).

Black velvet skirt

A piece of black velvet was cut into two lengths of 180 x 38cm (72 x 15in), to give a final skirt length of 90cm (35½in). Each length of velvet was sewn (separately) along the long edges and pushed on to a tube. After dyeing, they were discharged using method 2 and non-reducible dyes (see page 11). The two lengths were cut in half to give four 90cm (36in) panels. These were sewn together to form the skirt, leaving part of a side seam open as a slit. A lining of black crêpe de chine was sewn inside the skirt and an elasticated waist band was attached.

Arashi on silk

METHOD

1. Fold the silk in three, lengthwise (the photo shows a Georgette scarf 180 x 45cm (71 x 18in). Sew together the open long sides.

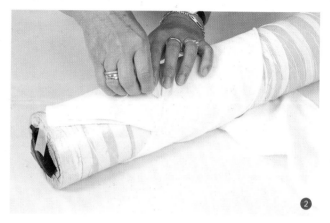

2. Use sticky tape to attach the top of the fabric strip to the tube. Now wind the folded fabric at an angle around the tube. Secure the folds of silk with tacking stitches.

3. Bunch the fabric gently to make small folds and then wind string around the length of the tube. Push the folds as close together as possible and secure with string.

4. (Not illustrated) Apply the required acid dye with a pipette and use a stiff paintbrush to spread it about. Use a pipette to apply a 50:50 solution of water and vinegar (see page 8). Place the tube into a saucepan fitted with a steaming basket. Press a piece of aluminium foil over the top to prevent steam from escaping, then steam for fifteen minutes (see also, Twisting, pages 16–17). Remove the scarf from the tube to reveal a stunning zig-zag pattern. Alternatively, if you want the fabric to remain tightly pleated, let the silk dry out thoroughly on the tube before removing it.

Georgette scarf
180 x 45cm (72 x 18in)

This scarf was dyed using various shades of green and blue, following the steps opposite. It was then boiled for eight minutes in a black dye bath and discharged using method 1 (see page 10).

VARIATION

As with the Twisting technique, you can follow the steps shown here but, before removing the fabric from the tube, boil for eight minutes in a black dye bath – use 80ml of dye per litre of water (1 ½fl.oz per pint). The fabric can then be discharged following method 1 on page 10.

Silk travelling rug
150 x 210cm (60 x 84in)

Three lengths of satin crêpe were cut out – two 200 x 20cm (80 x 8in) lengths for the edges and one 200 x 90cm (80 x 36in) length for the middle. Each length was dyed individually using acid dyes, following steps 1–3 on page 34. The dyes were applied with a firm brush, and care was taken to ensure that the spaces in between were coloured too. The fabric was allowed to dry thoroughly, before being removed from the tube and steam-fixed. The thin blue strips of fabric are 5cm (2in) wide and were cut from crêpe de chine. A piece of black quilted silk, 150 x 210cm (60 x 84in) was used for the underside of the rug.

Zig-zag pleated chiffon scarf
90 x 180cm (36 x 72in)

A totally different effect can be creating by one simple adjustment of the Arashi technique shown on page 34. After dyeing with acid dyes, this scarf was left on the tube and allowed to dry thoroughly before it was removed. It should not be washed as this will cause the pleating to disappear.

Crêpe de chine pareu
115 x 180cm (45 x 72in)

The pareu was tacked lengthwise along
the selvedges, then pushed on to a thick
tube, circumference 115cm (45in). It
was then dyed with acid dyes, following
steps 2–3 on page 34. When dry, it
was steam-fixed. The striking linear pattern
was then emphasised using gold outliner.

Georgette wall hanging
180 x 90cm (72 x 36in)

This wall hanging was dyed using acid
dyes, following steps 1–4 on page 34.
The silk was then boiled in a black dye
bath and discharged using method 1
shown on page 10.

Satin crêpe wall hanging
200 x 90cm (80 x 36in)

The fiery-coloured wall hanging in the left of this picture was dyed with acid dyes,
in exactly the same way as the scarf shown on page 37. The scarf on the right is
featured on the previous page.

Hand-pleated georgette skirt

This skirt would make a fabulous addition to any woman's wardrobe. The elastic was detached from the waistband of a ready-made white georgette skirt and the fabric was folded in four, lengthwise. It was dyed using acid dyes, as described on page 34, steps 1–4. The skirt was then boiled in a black dye bath and discharged using method 1. After removing it from the tube, it was washed, then twisted into a cord while still damp. The cord was placed in a 600-watt microwave for twenty minutes – this dried the fabric and also produced the pleating. When unwound, the elastic was threaded back in to complete the skirt.

41

MANDALA

A mandala is an original symbol of
Asiatic art. The pattern always
develops outwards from the centre of
the fabric. In shibori, you can create
your very own mandala by folding,
winding, binding and dyeing.
Amazingly, no two mandalas are ever
the same, because there is always a
touch of magic in shibori. In this
demonstration, I have used a piece of
silk pongé 06, 115cm (45in)
square and I have coloured it with
acid dyes, which is why vinegar is
used (see page 8)

METHOD

1. (Not illustrated) Iron a square
of silk then fold the fabric in half
and then half again to form a
smaller square.

2. Fold this square into a triangle,
ensuring that the folded centre of the
silk is at the apex of the triangle (this
is very important).

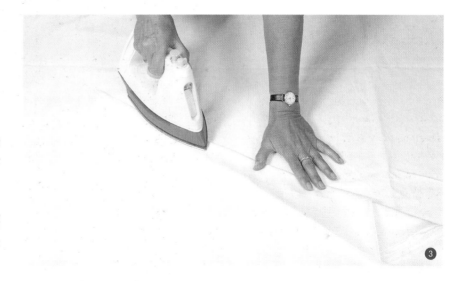

3. Keep the folded centre of the fabric at the apex, and fold once again to form a long narrow triangle. Iron in the folds.

Tip If you slightly dampen the top of the triangle, the folds will stay in place better.

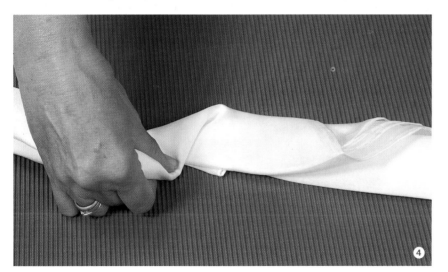

4. Place the triangle of fabric on your work surface, with the tip pointing to the right. Fold the triangle into a 'witches staircase'. To do this, place your left hand across the fabric, with your thumb and forefinger forming a right angle (Diagram 1). Now fold the tip of the triangle up over your hand (Diagram 2). Turn the fabric over and repeat, then turn it over again, and repeat once more.

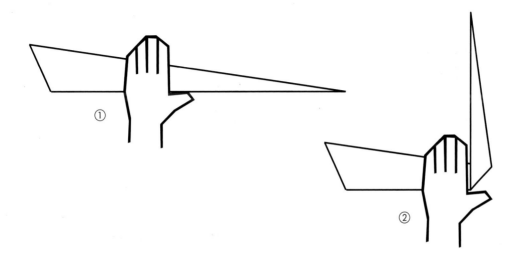

① ②

5. Hold the folded fabric in both hands and wrap it around your index and middle fingers.

6. Slowly withdraw your fingers. As you do so, twist the rest of the tip and then wrap it around itself to form a ball.

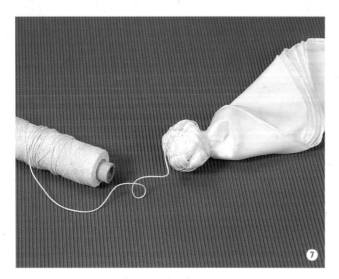

7. Wind string around the ball of fabric to secure it.

8. Use a pipette to apply between three and five colours of acid dye to the ball. Work over a plastic container as you do this, to catch any stray drips of dye.

9. (Not illustrated). Pour diluted vinegar over the ball and then interim steam-fix for fifteen minutes. To do this, add about 2.5cm (1in) of water to a saucepan fitted with a steaming basket in the bottom. Place the dyed ball of fabric inside, cover the pan with aluminium foil and steam for fifteen minutes (see Twisting, pages 16–17). Rinse the ball thoroughly under a tap, then boil for eight minutes in a black dye bath – use 80ml of dye per litre of water (1½fl.oz per pint). Remove the fabric and again, rinse thoroughly. Dry off on a towel and undo the string.

VARIATION

After the interim fixing you can boil the silk in any dark-coloured dye – dark blue often looks very effective.

10. Unfold the fabric to reveal a magnificently colourful mandala. Wash the fabric once more in water, then dry it and iron as normal.

Silk pongé shoulder throw (see also illustration on page 42)
115cm (45in) square

I used silk pongé 06 for this unusual throw. It was dyed using reactive dyes, following steps 1–10 on pages 42–45.

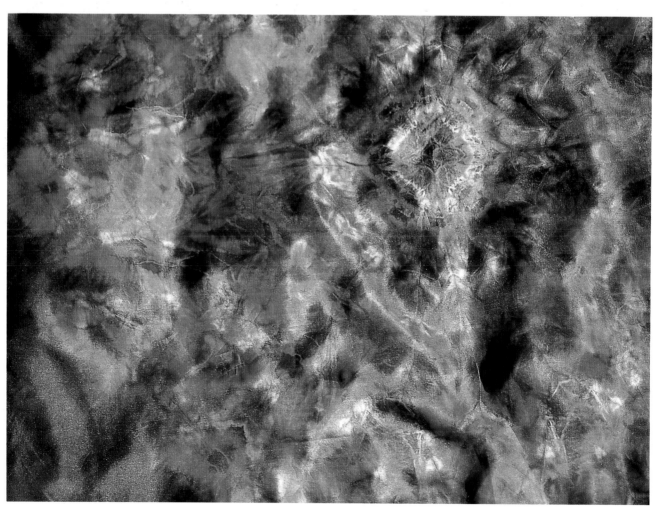

Woollen shoulder throw

120cm (48in) square

Vibrant colours can look even more spectacular when worked on a black background. This shoulder throw was dyed in the same way as the one shown opposite, but this time I used acid dyes.

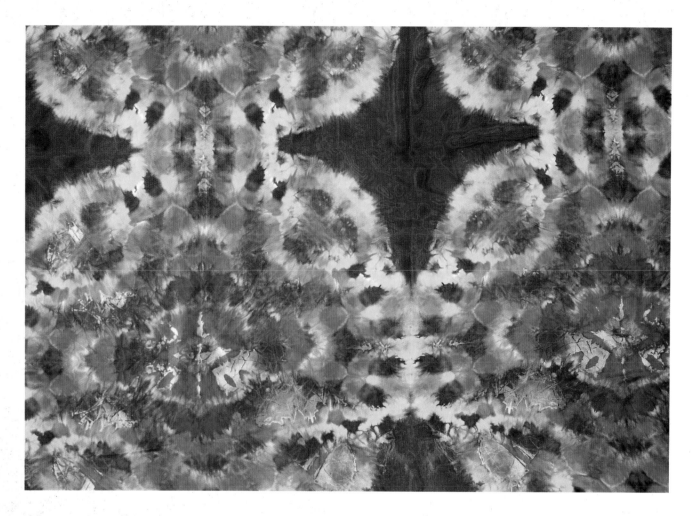

Silk pongé shoulder throw
120cm (48in) square

I have worked four mandalas on this brightly-coloured throw. A piece of silk pongé 06
was folded in half four times (see diagram) to form a 30cm (12in) square. This square
was then folded to make a triangle, and steps 4–10 (pages 43–45) were followed,
using acid dyes.

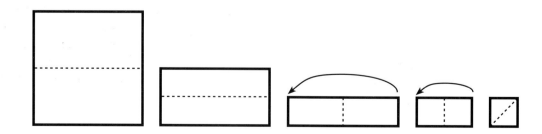

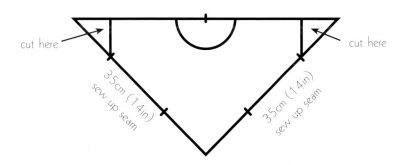

cut here → ← cut here

35cm (14in) sew up seam

35cm (14in) sew up seam

Triangular blouse

This mandala was worked on a 115cm (45in) square of pongé 06. It was dyed using reactive dyes. After following steps 1–10 on pages 42–45, the fabric was folded diagonally (see diagram). The neckline and sleeves were cut out, the neckline was edged with black silk, then the two side seams were sewn up.

MEANDER

The Meander technique takes its name from the intertwined, sinuous forms which result from it — these appear to wind across the fabric like a flowing river. With this shibori technique, small tacking stitches are worked on parts of the fabric, and these are then drawn together and bound tight. The result is a collection of soft patterns which run into one another. This demonstration is worked on a silk georgette scarf, 180 x 45cm (72 x 18in) and I have used acid dyes (see page 8).

METHOD

1. (Not illustrated) Iron your fabric thoroughly, then use an autofade marker to draw on three or so winding or curved lines.

2. Tack loosely along one of the marked lines. Now tighten the thread, to form the fabric into folds.

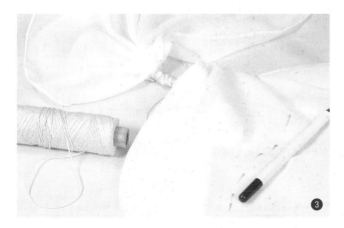

3. Bind the folds firmly with string. Repeat with the other lines. Bind corners as well, to produce more unusual patterns.

4. Place a plastic grid (available from art and craft shops) or a cake cooling rack over a plastic bowl or bucket. Position the silk on the grid and then drip acid dye over the fabric. Splash a 50:50 solution of vinegar and water over it.

5. Place the grid, with the silk still on top, over a saucepan containing boiling water. Cover with aluminium foil and steam for fifteen to twenty minutes.

6. (Not illustrated) Wash the silk under a tap, wring it out, undo the string and then iron.

Georgette scarf
180 x 90cm (72 x 36in)

The meander technique can be used to create a dramatic, flowing design that works perfectly on a scarf. The scarf was folded in half, lengthwise. It was then dyed using reactive dyes, following the steps on pages 50–51.

Woollen shoulder throw
120cm (48in) square

This stunning throw was dyed in the same way as the scarf opposite, but I used different colours.

Georgette scarf

180 x 90cm (72 x 36in)

This scarf was dyed using reactive dyes, following steps 1–5 on pages 50–51. It was then washed and dried gently with a towel. The fabric was wrapped from top to bottom with string and boiled for eight minutes in a black dye bath which had 80ml of dye per litre of water (1½fl.oz per pint). Step 6 was then worked to complete the scarf.

Georgette blouse

This silk blouse (also illustrated on page 50) was ready-made. It was buttoned up and an autofade marker was used to draw wavy lines over the fabric. It was unbuttoned and steps 2–5 on pages 50–51 were followed. Note: The colours (reactive dyes) were dripped on to the untied area only. After the interim fixing, the dyed areas were bound with string. The blouse was boiled for ten minutes in a black dye bath which had 80ml of dye per litre of water (1½fl.oz per pint). Step 6 completed the process.

ITAJIME

Itajime is a folding and pressing technique. The fabric is laid in accordion folds between two small boards, which are identical in shape. The fabric is then dyed to produce a fairly regular pattern.

For this technique, you can cut out the two boards yourself from wood — try using squares, circles, triangles or rectangles.

In this demonstration I have used silk pongé 06.

METHOD

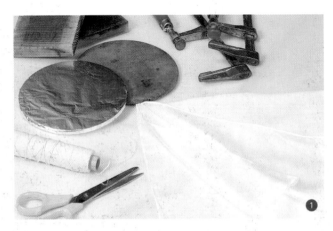

1. Form a large square of fabric into concertina folds to create a small square slightly larger than the boards.

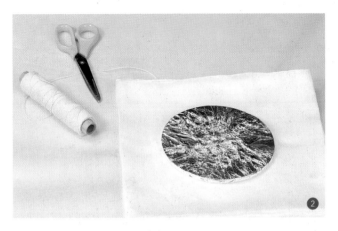

2. Cover the two identical boards with aluminium foil and place the folded silk between them.

3. Wind string around both boards, to catch in all the silk and to secure it in place. If you wish, you can squeeze the boards even closer together with clamps.

4. (Not illustrated) Make up a black dye bath in a saucepan — use 80ml of dye per litre of water (1½fl.oz per pint). Bring to the boil then immerse the boards in the dye. Boil for ten minutes then remove the boards. Rinse thoroughly, undo the string and, finally, iron the fabric.

Silk scarves
120cm (48in) square
90cm (36in) square

You do not always have to use lots of colour to create a striking effect. These two scarves were both dyed using only black dye. The design on the left was worked on pongé 06 using the technique shown opposite and round boards. The scarf on the right is pongé 05 and the design was created using rectangular boards.

Woollen scarf
55 x 200cm (22 x 80in)

The scarf was folded in three lengthwise and then folded accordion-style to form a square. Two shades of red dye were dripped on to the front and the back of the square, then steps 2–4 (page 56) were followed, using rectangular boards 11 x 8cm (4½ x 3in).

PLEATING

Pleating is a special type of shibori.
The fabric is formed into very fine
folds which, when dyed, produce
enchanting patterns on scarves,
clothing and wall hangings. Thin
chiffon silk is the most appropriate
fabric for this technique. In order to
achieve fine, tight folds, I use a small
smocking pleater with twenty-four
needles, available from specialist shops.

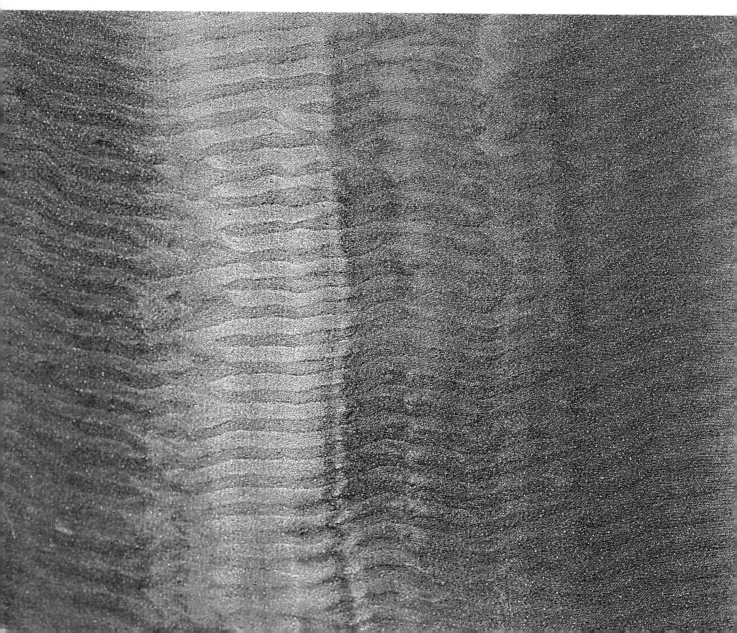

METHOD

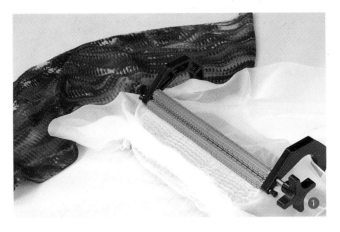

1. Thread each needle of a smocking pleater, then draw the fabric through the machine, leaving the threads hanging loose at the other end. Note: You may find it easier to fold a large item in half before drawing it through the machine.

2. Cut off the threads. Wrap the pleated silk securely around a small wooden dowel and then wind string around the dowel to hold the silk in place.

3. (Not illustrated) Use a pipette to drop acid dye and then a 50:50 solution of water and vinegar on to the fabric (see page 8). Add 2.5cm (1in) of water to the bottom of a saucepan. Place a steaming basket inside then lay the dyed fabric roll·on it. Place the saucepan on a hotplate, cover with aluminium foil and steam the fabric for twenty minutes. Wash the fabric roll in running water, towel dry, then remove the fabric from the dowel and undo the threads.

VARIATION

You can wait until the silk is thoroughly dry before you undo the threads. The pleating then remains intact.

Chiffon wall hanging
225 x 115cm (90 x 45in)

Pleating can often produce unexpected results. When I unfolded this piece, I decided to call it 'Thai dancer', because of the image that materialised at the bottom of the hanging. The fabric was folded in half lengthwise and then dyed with steam-fix dyes, following steps 1–3 on page 61. The wall hanging was lined with black wild silk and loops were added to the top edge. The curtain pole was covered with purple satin crêpe to complete the effect.

Chiffon scarf
180 x 45cm (72 x 18in)

Subtle autumnal colours have been used on this scarf (see also detail on page 60). The fabric was folded in half lengthwise and then dyed using acid dyes, following steps 1–3 on page 61. The silk was then bound on to the dowel again, and boiled briefly in a black dye bath which had 80ml of dye per litre of water (1½fl.oz per pint). It was discharged using method 1 (see page 10).

I would like to express my thanks to my colleague and friend, Inge Horak, for her help and support with the patterns that appear on pages 26, 32, 36, 37, 38, 47, 49, 55, 57 and 63.

~

First published in Great Britain 1999 by Search Press Limited
Wellwood, North Farm Road, Tunbridge Wells, Kent TN2 3DR

Reprinted 2000

Originally published in Germany 1998 by Augustus Verlag Augsburg

Original title: *Shibori: Seide Färben in Japanischer Tradition*

Copyright © Weltbild Verlag GmbH, 1998

English translation by Norman Porter

English translation copyright © Search Press Limited 1999

All rights reserved. No part of this book, text, photographs or illustrations may be reproduced or transmitted in any form or by any means by print, photoprint, microfilm, microfiche, photocopier internet or in any way known or as yet unknown, or stored in a retrieval system, without written permission obtained beforehand from Search Press.

ISBN 0 85532 895 9

Readers are permitted to reproduce any of the items/patterns in this book for their personal use, or for the purposes of selling for charity, free of charge and without the prior permission of the Publishers. Any use of the items/patterns for commercial purposes is not permitted without the prior permission of the Publishers.

The Publishers and author can accept no responsibility for any consequences arising from the information, advice or instructions given in this publication.

Suppliers
If you have difficulty in obtaining any of the materials and equipment mentioned in this book, then please write to the Publishers, at the address above, for a current list of stockists, including firms who operate a mail-order service.

Fringed velvet scarf

180 x 38cm (72 x 15in)

This fringed scarf (see also page 31) is made using the Arashi technique featured on pages 22–23.

Printed in Hong Kong by Bookbuilders